D1712664

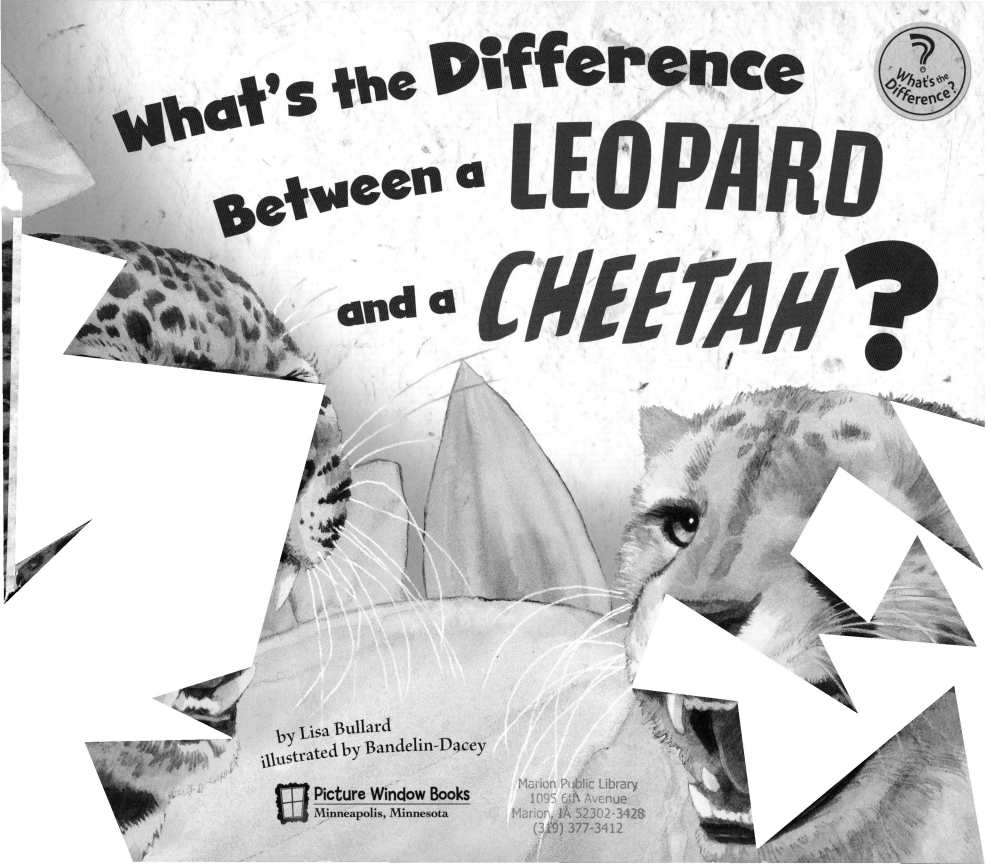

What's the Difference Between a LEOPARD and a CHEETAH?

by Lisa Bullard

illustrated by Bandelin-Dacey

Picture Window Books
Minneapolis, Minnesota

Leopards and cheetahs are two large members of the cat family. The two wild predators have many things in common.

For Katherine, great friend to me and to my own big cats

Thanks to our advisers for their expertise, research, and advice:

Blaire Van Valkenburgh, Ph.D.
Department of Ecology and Evolutionary Biology
University of California, Los Angeles

Terry Flaherty, Ph.D., Professor of English
Minnesota State University, Mankato

Editor: Shelly Lyons
Designer: Abbey Fitzgerald
Page Production: Melissa Kes
Art Director: Nathan Gassman
Editorial Director: Nick Healy
Creative Director: Joe Ewest
The illustrations in this book were created with watercolor.

Photo Credit: Shutterstock/siloto (handmade paper), 1 and
22 (background) and throughout in sidebars and titlebars.

Picture Window Books
151 Good Counsel Drive
P.O. Box 669
Mankato, MN 56002-0669
877-845-8392
www.picturewindowbooks.com

Copyright © 2010 by Picture Window Books

Printed in the United States of America.

 All books published by Picture Window Books
are manufactured with paper containing at least
10 percent post-consumer waste.

Library of Congress Cataloging-in-Publication Data
Bullard, Lisa.
What's the difference between a leopard and a cheetah? / by Lisa B
illustrated by Bandelin-Dacey.
p. cm. — (What's the difference?)
Includes index.
ISBN 978-1-4048-5548-9 (library binding)
1. Leopard—Juvenile literature. 2. Cheetah—Juvenile litera
I. Bandelin, Debra, ill. II. Dacey, Bob, ill. III. Title.
QL737.C23B85 2010
599.75'54—dc22   2009006886

But do you know the differences between a leopard and a cheetah?

Leopards and cheetahs are similar in size.

But leopards have heavier muscles that make them more powerful than cheetahs. In fights between these two cats, leopards almost always win.

Cheetahs have longer legs, longer backs, smaller heads, and thinner bodies than leopards. Cheetahs are built for speed.

Leopards and cheetahs grow to be about 3.3 to 4.6 feet (1 to 1.4 meters) long, not including the tail. An adult leopard weighs 62 to 200 pounds (27.9 to 90 kilograms). Full-grown cheetahs weigh 75 to 145 pounds (33.8 to 65.3 kg).

leopard

cheetah

Leopards and cheetahs both have light-colored fur with dark spots.

A leopard's spots are called rosettes. They are shaped like small flowers.

A cheetah's spots are solid black and usually rounded.

Many kinds of cats have spotted coats. The mix of colors helps them stay hidden when they are hunting prey.

Leopards and cheetahs hunt for their food. Leopards rely on their stalking ability. They creep as close to the prey as they can and then pounce.

Leopards can run in short bursts at about 36 miles (57.6 km) per hour.

Cheetahs rely on their speed when hunting. They are the fastest animals on land. For cheetahs, their most important hunting tool is their great speed.

Estimates say that cheetahs can run as fast as 70 miles (112 km) per hour. But they can continue their top speed for only a short time.

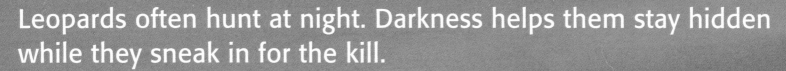

Leopards often hunt at night. Darkness helps them stay hidden while they sneak in for the kill.

Cheetahs usually hunt by day. Sunlight makes it easier for cheetahs to see the prey they race after. It also helps them avoid other predators such as leopards and lions.

Leopards and cheetahs both have excellent eyesight. Their eyes are among their most important hunting tools.

Leopards and cheetahs risk having their dinner stolen by other large meat-eaters, such as hyenas. To avoid this, leopards often drag their food high into trees. They are strong enough to haul up even very large animals.

Cheetahs try to eat as quickly as possible, before they lose their meal to other animals.

After a high-speed chase, a cheetah must rest for a few minutes. The animal must catch its breath before it can eat.

Leopards have long, sharp claws. Their claws are retractable. That means the claws draw into the paws when they aren't needed. This way, the claws stay sharp for hunting and climbing.

14

Cheetahs have shorter claws. Their claws do not draw all the way into their paws. Cheetahs use their claws to grip the ground when they speed along. The claws act like the spikes on some sports shoes.

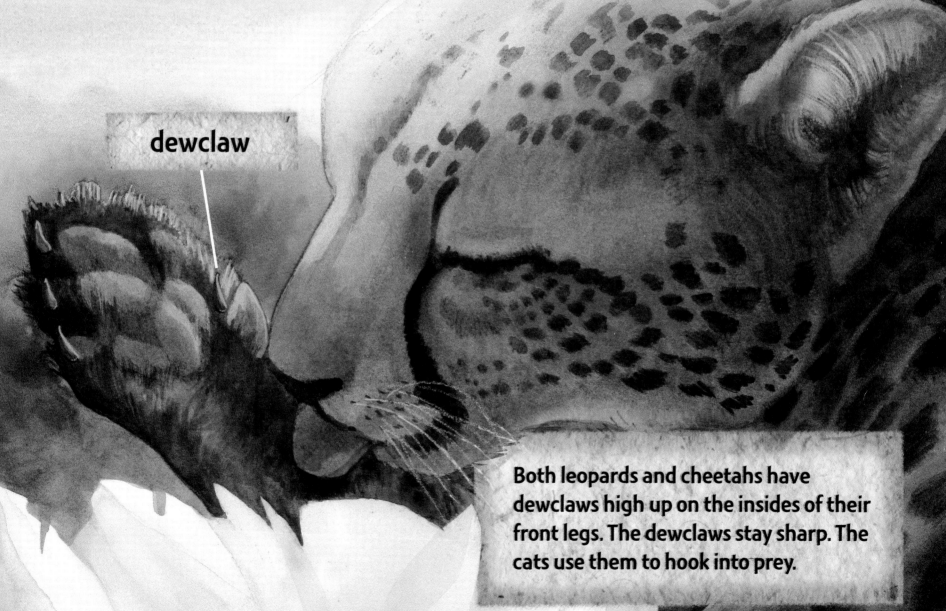

dewclaw

Both leopards and cheetahs have dewclaws high up on the insides of their front legs. The dewclaws stay sharp. The cats use them to hook into prey.

Look closely at the faces of these two large cats. The leopard has spots all over its face.

The cheetah has some spots on its face, too. But it also has dark lines running from the corners of its eyes to the corners of its mouth. The lines look like dark tear marks.

Some scientists believe a cheetah's dark tear marks help keep the sun's glare out of the animal's eyes during daytime hunts.

Leopards and cheetahs use sounds to communicate with other animals. They call out to their cubs, and hiss or snarl when threatened. But these wild cats do not make all the same noises.

Leopards can roar.

Cheetahs can't roar. Instead, they make a birdlike chirping sound. They also purr like house cats.

Members of the cat family also communicate with scent marks. Leopards and cheetahs may leave their scent by spraying urine on an object.

Adult female leopards and cheetahs live alone, except when they have cubs. Then the mother will live with her young. Adult male leopards live alone, too.

But adult male cheetahs sometimes live together in groups of two or three. These groups are called coalitions. Males born from the same female cheetah will often form a coalition.

Coalitions of male cheetahs can hunt larger prey, such as antelope and wildebeests. The coalition works together as a team while hunting.

LEOPARD

muscular body

rosettes

large head

excellent eyesight

roaring sounds

retractable claws

short legs

thin body

small head

CHEETAH

long legs

excellent eyesight

dark lines

solid spots

short claws that don't fully retract

chirping or purring sounds

22

Fun Facts

Some leopards have black instead of tan fur. The black rosettes are much harder to see, but look carefully! You will find they are still there.

Leopards are good athletes. They are some of the cat world's best tree climbers and are also good swimmers.

Leopards can be found living in more places in the world than any other wild cat.

Cheetah cubs have long gray fur that covers the top of their heads, the back of their necks, and their backs. This fur is called a mantle. It goes away as the cubs grow.

King cheetahs have a different pattern on their coats. Their spots join together to create stripes and odd shapes.

Glossary

coalition—a group of male cheetahs or male lions that live together

dewclaw—a claw found higher up on the leg; the claw does not reach the ground

pounce—to spring forward suddenly and attack

predator—an animal that hunts and eats other animals

prey—an animal that is hunted and eaten for food

retractable—able to retract or be pulled in

rosette—a flowerlike marking

scent mark—a smell that animals leave behind to communicate with other animals

stalk—to hunt an animal slowly

To Learn More

More Books to Read

Clarke, Ginjer L. *Cheetah Cubs*. New York: Grosset & Dunlap, 2007.

Landau, Elaine. *Big Cats: Hunters of the Night*. Berkeley Heights, N.J.: Enslow Elementary, 2008.

Patent, Dorothy Hinshaw. *Big Cats*. New York: Walker & Co., 2005.

Squire, Ann O. *Leopards*. New York: Children's Press, 2005.

Internet Sites

FactHound offers a safe, fun way to find Internet sites related to this book. All of the sites on FactHound have been researched by our staff.

Here's all you do:

Visit *www.facthound.com*

FactHound will fetch the best sites for you!

Index

Look for all of the books in the What's the Difference? series:

What's the Difference Between a Butterfly and a Moth?

What's the Difference Between a Frog and a Toad?

What's the Difference Between a Leopard and a Cheetah?

What's the Difference Between an Alligator and a Crocodile?